HISTORY IN LITERATURE

THE STORY BEHIND...

JOHN STEINBECK'S

OF MICE AND MEN

Brian Williams

Heinemann
LIBRARY

www.heinemann.co.uk/library
Visit our website to find out more information about Heinemann Library books.

To order:

 Phone 44 (0) 1865 888066

 Send a fax to 44 (0) 1865 314091

 Visit the Heinemann Bookshop at www.heinemann.co.uk/library to browse our catalogue and order online.

First published in Great Britain by
Heinemann Library, Halley Court, Jordan Hill,
Oxford, OX2 8EJ, part of Harcourt
Education. Heinemann is a registered
trademark of Harcourt Education Ltd.

© Harcourt Education Ltd 2007
First published in paperback in 2008
The moral right of the proprietor has been
asserted.

Editorial: Louise Galpine, Lucy Beevor,
and Rosie Gordon
Design: Richard Parker
and Manhattan Design
Picture Research: Melissa Allison
and Elaine Willis
Production: Vicki Fitzgerald
Originated by Modern Age
Printed and bound in China by Leo Paper Group

13 digit ISBN: 978 0 431 08172 4 (hardback)
11 10 09 08 07
10 9 8 7 6 5 4 3 2 1

13 digit ISBN: 978 0 431 08189 2 (paperback)
12 11 10 09 08
10 9 8 7 6 5 4 3 2 1

British Library Cataloguing in Publication Data
Williams, Brian, 1943-
The story behind Of mice and
men. - (History in literature)
813.5'2
A full catalogue record for this book is
available from the British Library.

Acknowledgements
The author and publishers are grateful to the
following for permission to reproduce copyright
photographs/quotes: **p. 31**, akg-images; **p. 46**,
Alamy/POPPERFOTO; **pp. 16, 17, 32, 24**,
CORBIS; **p. 45**, Corbis Sygma/COOPER ANDREW;
p. 12, Corbis/ American Gothic, 1930 by Grant
Wood, All rights reserved by the Estate of Nan
Wood Graham/Licensed by VAGA, New York, NY;
**pp. 14, 15, 20, 21, 22, 42, 36, 26, 27, 25, 44, 47,
49, 38**, CORBIS/Bettmann; **p. 35**, CORBIS/
Dorothea Lange; **p. 33**, CORBIS/H. Armstrong
Roberts; **p. 41**, CORBIS/Hulton-Deutsch
Collection; **p. 5**, CORBIS/Philip James Corwin; **p.
48**, CORBIS/ Ted Streshinsky; **p. 10**, CORBIS/
Underwood & Underwood; **p. 8**, Getty Images/
Anthony Potter Collection; **p. 11**, Getty Images/
Frank Driggs Collection; **pp. 4, 9, 18**, Getty
Images/Hulton Archive; **pp. 7, 40**, Getty Images/
Keystone; **p. 9**, Getty Images/Time Life Pictures/
Arthur Schatz; **p. 37**, Getty Images/Time Life
Pictures/Eric Schaal; **p. 34**, Getty Images/Time
Life Pictures/Margaret Bourke-White; **pp. 28,
29**, Image courtesy of The Advertising Archives;
p. 39, Mary Evans/Explorer Archives; **p. 23**, The
Kobal Collection/20th Century Fox; **p. 43**, The
Penguin Collectors Society; **p. 18**, Topfoto; **p. 30**,
UCL Library Services, Special Collections, Orwell
Archives. **Cover**: Corbis/Bettman.

Excerpts from Of Mice and Men by John
Steinbeck, copyright 1937, renewed © 1965 by
John Steinbeck. Used by permission of Penguin
Group UK and Viking Penguin, a division of
Penguin Group (USA) Inc

The publishers would like to thank Dr Barbara
Heavilin for her assistance in the preparation of
this book.

Every effort has been made to contact copyright
holders of any material reproduced in this book.
Any omissions will be rectified in subsequent
printings if notice is given to the publishers.

Disclaimer

Contents

Some words are shown in bold, **like this**. You can find out what they mean by looking in the glossary.

Steinbeck's life and times

John Steinbeck was one of the most successful US writers of the 1900s. His career was crowned in 1962 with the award of the **Nobel Prize** for Literature. *Of Mice and Men*, published in 1937, is set in rural America during the **Depression**, and is about a pair of **migrant** farmworkers clinging to a dream that one day they will have a farm of their own. Steinbeck explored a similar theme in his next novel, *The Grapes of Wrath*, which tells of a poor Oklahoma migrant family hoping to find work in California.

The Golden State

The dream of California motivates many of Steinbeck's characters. California is known as the "Golden State". Its climate is sunny and its soil is fertile. The rapid growth of California as a US state began in 1848–1849 when gold-seekers poured in hoping to "strike it rich" during the "Gold Rush". In the year after gold was discovered, California's population grew by ten times to over 100,000. Today, the state has a population of 33 million. Modern California has hi-tech industries, such as computers and aerospace, but it is also the leading US agricultural state. Many farms still hire migrant workers like the two men Steinbeck wrote about in *Of Mice and Men*.

Steinbeck was sensitive about his appearance. His sisters nicknamed him "mouse" because of his large ears and nose. He was also sensitive about his reputation. Although he went on writing into the 1960s he felt some critics praised only his 1930s books.

BOOM STATE

*California has four of the United States' biggest cities: Los Angeles, San Diego, San Jose, and San Francisco. Los Angeles grew from a city of 100,000 in 1900 to 1.5 million by 1945. Its population is now around 3.8 million. Modern California is famous for the electronics of **Silicon Valley**, but also for its huge production of fruit and vegetables (such as grapes, oranges, nuts, lettuce, and tomatoes), field crops (such as cotton, corn, and sugar beet), and dairy products (such as butter and cheese).*

Steinbeck was born in 1912 in this solidly middle-class house on Central Avenue, Salinas. He lived here until the age of seventeen.

Steinbeck's California

Today, more than 90 per cent of Californians live in cities. In 1902, when John Steinbeck was born, most people in the state lived on farms or in small country towns. Steinbeck was raised in Salinas, a town of around 2,500 people in a valley in central California, south of San Francisco. *Of Mice and Men* begins with a poetic description of a landscape he loved: of the Salinas River running "deep and green", and wildlife including lizards, rabbits, raccoons, deer, and a water snake. Into this beautiful landscape come George and Lennie, the two men who are the central characters in Steinbeck's story.

Of Mice and Men can seem like a simple book, but the story is powerful and the characters are drawn in a way that shows how people lived in rural America just before World War II (1939–1945).

Steinbeck grew up in "small-town" America, where most people helped one another, just as George looks out for Lennie in the novel.

> *People pulled together in those days ... we realized that if one man fell, everyone would fall ...*

This was how one Salinas resident recalled life in the early 1900s.

This map shows the state of California (and United States, inset) where Steinbeck spent much of his life, and where *Of Mice and Men* is set.

Growing up in California

Steinbeck's parents, John Ernst and Olive Hamilton Steinbeck, were respectable citizens of Salinas. Mr Steinbeck had not succeeded in business on his own, but a safe accounting job at Spreckels Sugar Plant gave him a regular income. Mrs Steinbeck was more ambitious, especially for her son John who was the third of her four children. In 1906, when John was four he was taken to see buildings in the town shaken by the earthquake that had destroyed San Francisco. His mother encouraged John to read. His parents were keen that he should become a scientist. But John loved the tales of *King Arthur* and his knights, and at school showed a talent for storytelling. Another interest was marine life, which he studied while wandering the beaches around the family's weekend cottage near Monterey.

Deciding to be a writer

After graduating from high school in 1919, Steinbeck went to college at Stanford. He left without a degree, and in 1925 headed east to try his luck in New York City as a construction worker, and then as a reporter – until he was fired. He hoped to sell stories, but a year later he was back in California. He moved into a cabin at Lake Tahoe, working as an odd-job man, watching wildlife, and writing.

Boom and bust

In the 1920s, the United States experienced a **consumer boom**. People bought goods on "instalment plans" and invested in **stocks**. Banks lent too much money and by 1929, too many people were spending more money than they could earn. When prices on New York's Wall Street Stock Exchange collapsed, millions of people lost their savings. The **Wall Street Crash** of 1929 marked the start of the Depression. Businesses closed, workers lost their jobs, and farm prices tumbled. Environmental disaster made things worse for farmers hit by the Depression. Between 1935 and 1938, fierce storms hit the parched prairie grasslands of the United States, which was overused for grazing cattle and growing wheat. The winds whipped off thin, parched soil in clouds of dust creating the **Dust Bowl**.

Finding inspiration in bad times

After an unsuccessful attempt at historical fiction with *Cup of Gold*, a novel about pirates of the 1600s, Steinbeck found his real inspiration in the mid–1930s. Writing about people struggling through the Depression, he tried to work in themes from the King Arthur stories he loved. His first success, *Tortilla Flat*, is about a group of "down-and-outs" living together in Monterey. Steinbeck likened them to King Arthur's knights because they stick together. *Of Mice and Men* is the second of three novels he wrote about farmworkers: *In Dubious Battle* is about a workers' **strike** and *The Grapes of Wrath* is about families trekking to the "promised land" of California.

A migrant family, one of thousands looking for a new life in America during the 1930s Depression. Bleak images like this photograph shocked a nation.

The story unfolds . . .

In the novel, George Milton and Lennie Small have come to work at a ranch in the Salinas Valley. George complains about the bus driver who dropped them miles from the gate, while Lennie worries about the dead mouse in his pocket. George throws the mouse away, warning Lennie not to speak to anybody at the ranch. Lennie, it is clear, often gets them both into trouble.

The dream future

Lennie is a child in a man's body. He is innocent, and does not know his own strength: he wants to pet the mouse, but he kills it. George looks after him. The pair had to leave their previous jobs in a hurry, after a woman accused Lennie of assaulting her. As they make camp for the night, George tells Lennie a familiar "bedtime story". It is the story of their dream future when they will own a farm, and Lennie will have rabbits to look after.

In the **bunkhouse**, George and Lennie meet the **ranch hands**. Among them are: the skinner (mule-driver) Slim; the ageing crippled "swamper" (cleaner and odd-job man) Candy; and the African-American "stable-buck" Crooks. They also meet the boss's son Curley, and Curley's bored wife. Lennie is given a puppy by Slim. When Candy hears about George and Lennie's dream for the future, he offers them his savings for a share in the farm.

Ranch hands in a bunkhouse. Steinbeck had met many men like George and Lennie, with bundles on their backs, tramping from one ranch to the next, looking for work.

TRAMPING FOR WORK

Across the United States, and in Europe, millions of people were made penniless by the Depression. In the cities, "soup kitchens" served free food to lines of hungry people. In 1936, jobless men walked 300 miles from Jarrow, in north-east England, to London to draw attention to unemployment. The Jarrow "hunger marches" made people realize how bad things were in the industrial north.

The dream is shattered

The aggressive Curley **goads** Lennie into a fight. When he fights back, Lennie crushes Curley's hand, but the other men agree not to get him into trouble. Later, Crooks teases Lennie about the dream and says it will never come true. Next day, Lennie kills his pup by "petting" it too roughly. Then, Curley's wife corners him and tells him of her dream of becoming a movie star. Teasing him, she asks Lennie to stroke her hair, but he strokes too roughly. She screams and, in his panic, Lennie tries to silence her and accidently breaks her neck.

Lennie runs away, and is hunted by Curley and the others with guns. George finds his friend by the pool where the story began, and Lennie admits, "I done another bad thing." George tells him the dream story about the farm and the rabbits for the last time, before shooting Lennie to save him from prison or hanging.

Lennie's last words are "Le's get that place now." The other men arrive, drawn by the sound of the shot, and Slim reassures George that he did the only thing he could.

The poet Robert Burns (1759-1796), Scotland's national poet, was a farmer as well as a writer.

> ## The best laid schemes o' mice an' men/
> ## Gang aft a-gley

This is a quotation from the poem "To a Mouse" by the Scottish poet Robert Burns who knew the uncertainties of life as a farmer. His message is that plans do not always work out ("gang aft a-gley" means "often go wrong"), and it gave Steinbeck the title for his novel.

Post-war politics

Writers of the 1930s were very aware of politics and issues such as strikes, unemployment, the **class struggle** between rich and poor, and the arguments between **communists** and non-communists. The world had not been at peace for very long since the end of World War I (1914–1918). This war was helped toward an end by the arrival of US troops in Europe in 1917. When the troops came home, the US government withdrew into "isolation" from European affairs. This was a popular policy with many Americans who wanted no more foreign wars.

Writer of the Jazz Age

The most famous US writer of the 1920s was F. Scott Fitzgerald, known as the novelist of the "Jazz Age". Fitzgerald liked smart people, fast cars, city parties, and "hot music". He made the most of his fame and went to Hollywood to write for films. Steinbeck however wanted to write about California's "forgotten people", and their hard-working lives.

Scott and Zelda Fitzgerald knew California as a glamorous, glittering movie world: not the world of farmers and ranchers that Steinbeck wrote about in *Of Mice and Men*.

WRITERS OF THE TIME

US novelists writing at the same time as Steinbeck (with an example of one of their books) included:

- *F. Scott Fitzgerald (1896–1940)*   *The Great Gatsby*
- *John Dos Passos (1896–1970)*   *U.S.A.*
- *William Faulkner (1897–1962)*   *The Sound and the Fury*
- *Ernest Hemingway (1899–1961)*   *A Farewell to Arms*
- *Richard Wright (1908–1960)*   *Native Son*
- *Eudora Welty (1909–2001)*   *The Optimist's Daughter*

THE ROARING TWENTIES

*The Roaring Twenties was a term used to describe the post-war decade when society became more free and easy. These were the years of skirts that revealed women's knees, the Charleston dance, the romantic silent film star Rudolph Valentino, radio, jazz bands, and the first successful "talking film", The Jazz Singer. But it was not all fun. The 1920s also saw **Prohibition**, gangsters, a general (national) strike by workers in Britain in 1926, and the Wall Street Crash of 1929.*

The Cotton Club was a night club in New York City, famous for its jazz musicians and dancers.

Writers in and out of the United States

Some US writers, like Steinbeck, wrote mainly about everyday life in the United States. Some poked fun at small-town ways, as Sinclair Lewis did in his 1920 novel *Main Street*. Writers who had fought in World War I, such as novelists John Dos Passos and Ernest Hemingway, drew on their wartime experiences. Hemingway moved to Europe, and he was not alone among US writers and artists in looking for fresh ideas abroad.

As a young man Steinbeck, too, had dreamed of exploring the world, but he only travelled as far as New York City. He did not belong to what the Paris-based writer Gertude Stein called the "Lost Generation" of writers who felt out of step with 1920s US society and went to Europe for inspiration. Steinbeck did not visit Europe until 1937, after *Of Mice and Men* had been published.

What motivated Steinbeck?

Steinbeck never had a steady job outside of writing. Until the mid-1930s, when his books began to sell well, he relied for income on his parents and the wages of his first wife Carol. The young couple lived in the Steinbeck family vacation cottage at Pacific Grove on the coast near Monterey. Carol got interested in **left-wing** protest politics, but John usually preferred having a few drinks with male friends, or walking along the shore and valleys watching nature.

Breakthrough

Steinbeck's first three books had not sold well, and on reading the **manuscript** of the fourth book, *Tortilla Flat*, his publisher said it made no sense. Fortunately, another publisher, Pascal (Pat) Covici, agreed to take *Tortilla Flat*, and further books. For Steinbeck, 1935 was a breakthrough year. He sold the film rights of *Tortilla Flat* for US$4,000, which meant he could build his own country home at Los Gatos. There, sitting at a desk with a view of a canyon, he wrote *Of Mice and Men*.

American Gothic by Grant Wood was painted in 1930. It shows an American farmer and his daughter. Like Steinbeck, Wood focused on rural America, looking at conditions there in a harsh, realistic light.

JUST ANOTHER JOB

In a letter to a friend in 1933, Steinbeck said he knew he "was not the material of which great artists were made". Writing was work, like carpentry or digging ditches: "I have a book to write. I think about it for a while and then I write it. There is nothing more." In April 1936 he wrote, "The work I am doing now is neither a novel nor a play, but it is a kind of playable novel." After his puppy Toby chewed up half the pages, Steinbeck spent two months rewriting the Of Mice and Men manuscript, before it was sent to the publisher.

Ideals and income

Writers have to earn a living, but Steinbeck suspected that *Of Mice and Men* would not make him rich. It was too short, too simple, and not political enough. Steinbeck wanted to write a good story, about innocence and hope, in a true-to-life way.

Many writers of the time used books to talk about their politics. Their stories showed the ugly side of life, and the writers used the stories to argue political causes.

Steinbeck hoped *Of Mice and Men* would open readers' eyes to the lives of poor **bindlestiffs**. He also wanted it to be a timeless tale about how people live, and a story with a message.

After finishing *Of Mice and Men*, Steinbeck drove off in an old truck into the countryside. During this trip, he visited a camp for migrant workers. Known as "Weedpatch", its tents were crammed with men, women, and children. He called these people "The Harvest Gypsies". The experience gave him ideas for his next book, *The Grapes of Wrath*.

Films in the 1930s brought excitement and escape in the form of comedies, westerns, gangster thrillers, historical epics, and musicals. The lavish musical shows staged by Busby Berkeley took audiences into a glitzy world that was like a fairy tale compared with their everyday experience.

THE PROMISED LAND

*Between 1860 and 1930, the population of the United States had risen
from 31 million to 123 million. For millions of **immigrants**, the United
States was the "promised land". By the 1920s, the United States was
the richest nation in the world. It was a land of skyscrapers, cars, and
luxuries, such as washing machines and vacuum cleaners. Then came
the Depression of the 1930s.*

A temporary halt?

In 1929, the Wall Street Crash hit the world economy. Banks failed and businesses
collapsed. People lost their life-savings overnight. Workers were thrown out of their
jobs. Steinbeck saw how badly the Depression that followed the Crash hit
California's farmers. Farm prices sank so low that many farmers were ruined. US
President Hoover called the Depression "a temporary halt in the **prosperity** of a
great people", but soon the US government was forced to help farmers and fund
new job-creation projects such as the construction of the Hoover Dam on the
Colorado River.

President Herbert Hoover promised that "prosperity is just around
the corner", but by 1932 more than 12 million Americans were out of
work. Homeless families found shelter in ramshackle shanty towns like
this, which became known as "Hoovervilles".

The United States in the Depression

Life in the 1920s and 1930s was tough for many people. Prohibition in the United States led to law-breaking, illegal drinking, and, in cities like Chicago, gang warfare between mobsters fighting for control of the illegal drinks business. Factories were becoming more important than farms, and the car worker was replacing the cowboy as a symbol of the American working man. Politicians praised the "rugged individualism" of Americans, but this often meant the weak were trodden underfoot by the strong.

Unemployed people in the US wait their turn on the bread line in a 1930s emergency food station.

"BUDDY, CAN YOU SPARE A DIME?"

"Buddy, Can You Spare a Dime?" was a 1931 song. It had the sad message that men who had fought in the war, and been proud to build bridges and railroads now had to beg for spare change. Old work songs about heroic railroad workers, were joined by new protest songs, such as those of folk singer Woody Guthrie from Oklahoma, who sang about "down and outs" on the road.

This land could be your land

Most ordinary people struggled on, without help, hoping for better times, like the two bindlestiffs in *Of Mice and Men*, who tramp the roads with bundles on their backs. George and Lennie are good workers. They can cut barley, tend livestock, and load a wagon. Their skills, however, earn them very little. Each week's work provides a bed, food, and a few dollars to spend or to save towards their dream of becoming their own bosses.

California awakening

Steinbeck's Californian background gave him a lot of material for writing *Of Mice and Men*. His sister Beth remembered that after each day's vacation work as a ranch hand, young John came home exhausted, but "full of stories" to tell around the kitchen table. This experience showed him how tough life was for the likes of George and Lennie.

Work experience

Steinbeck was strong and fit, but he found farm work exhausting. He and his college friend George Mors sweated on Spreckels Sugar Company beet farms and cattle ranches in the Salinas Valley. There he met his first bindlestiffs. Like George and Lennie, they did any work that was going, such as feeding pigs, cutting corn, digging wells, picking apples, and mending fences.

Horses used to bring in the harvest. By the 1930s, farmers were switching to machines. This meant they needed only five or six men at harvest time. A generation before, 100 workers might have been hired.

Life choices

Steinbeck might have chosen a "safe" career, perhaps in science. Instead he studied arts at college, left with no degree, got fired as a reporter, worked on building sites, and all the time insisted he would make it as a writer. His choices must have worried his family, especially considering the financial uncertainty of the times. Like most writers, Steinbeck absorbed what he saw. He said, "I was a bindlestiff myself for quite a spell, I worked in the same country that the story is laid in".

He also said he had once seen a man, like Lennie, stab a foreman with a pitchfork. This may, or may not, be true. Steinbeck said that Lennie and George were "composites" (mixtures) of people he had met. Steinbeck was impressed by the humour and patience of the bindlestiffs, but saw that their lives were often lonely. "They just come in and work a month and then they quit . . . Never seem to give a damn about nobody", says Slim, the top ranch hand in *Of Mice and Men.*

A field worker picking cotton. The cotton plantations in America were hard-hit by the Depression of the 1930s, and demand for workers fell. Today machines harvest the cotton.

Times change

By the 1930s, farm machines could harvest crops more quickly than people could, and tractors were replacing horses. Migrant workers were no longer wanted. As the Depression got worse, farmers first fired men like Candy, who is old and has lost a hand. He knows he will be the first to go. So, like George and Lennie, he dreams of a farm of his own. That would mean security, and hope that the Depression years might be over.

California, here we come

California was still the promised land for many, including poor families from Mexico. California's farms still relied on cheap labour at harvest time, and each year "economic migrants" moved through small towns like Salinas looking for their next job. There were families in rusting trucks, and men, alone or in pairs for company, walking or riding buses and freight trains. Wandering workmen or "tramps" were often seen in Britain, too. As late as the 1950s poor London families travelled out of the city into the countryside to pick fruit at harvest time, for a summer holiday with pay.

MIGRANTS IN THE PROMISED LAND

George describes his dream future in Of Mice and Men: ". . . we'd have a little house an' a room to ourself. Little fat iron stove, an' in the winter we'd keep a fire goin' in it . . . We wouldn't have to buck no barley eleven hours a day."

"A little house", like the one George dreams of, was part of the "American dream"; the dream that had drawn millions of immigrants to the United States. In the 1930s there was a fresh movement of people across the United States, mainly towards the west coast, particularly California, looking for a better life.

The union movement

Workers like George and Lennie seldom joined **trade unions**. In *Of Mice and Men*, George grumbles about money, but he and Lennie must accept the wages the boss offers, or move on. Union leaders tried, often without success, to organize farmworkers. Some farm owners were convinced that union supporters spread **socialist** ideas. They did not want to pay higher wages and even feared socialist groups would take over private farms. Steinbeck saw union efforts for himself. In California, he'd met Cicil McKiddy, from Oklahoma, a union man who handed out leaflets and tried to recruit new members.

By the 1930s, trade unions were growing stronger. In May 1926, British workers staged a General Strike. The army and police had to do some of the workers' jobs during the nine-day strike.

Farmworkers united

The bindlestiffs were mostly poor whites and Mexicans. Steinbeck's first wife Carol met many such workers in her work for the **Emergency Relief Organization** set up by President Roosevelt. Steinbeck sympathised with the workers, and approved when Roosevelt brought in new laws to strengthen union rights, and set up a National Labour Relations Board to improve conditions for workers. Most US migrant farm workers, however, remained non-unionized until the 1960s when Mexican-American labour leader Cesar Chavez organized the National Farm Workers Association, which became the United Farm Workers (UFW) in 1972.

Cesar Chavez (1927–1993) came from an Arizona family of migrant farm workers. He became a union organizer, and was elected president of the United Farm Workers of America.

BOSSES AND FAT CATS

*The ranch boss in Of Mice and Men is good-natured, but some bosses were **tyrants**. Before the Depression, most Americans had admired business leaders, such as Andrew Carnegie, the steel boss who gave millions of dollars to good causes. Union leaders were often described as crooks or communists. After the 1929 Wall Street Crash, people were more in favour of unions, and more suspicious of rich "fat cat" bosses.*

The American dream

The American dream was based on the belief that any person could succeed in the United States through his or her own efforts. This idea was based on hard work and self-sufficiency, and inspired the **pioneers** who went West in the 1800s. Some prospered, but many did not. The successful few inspired others. George and Lennie have never saved enough money to buy their dream farm, until they meet Candy at the ranch. Candy knows he is lucky to be kept on by a good-natured boss. He feels he is living on borrowed time.

He compares himself to his old dog, shot when it becomes too smelly for the bunkhouse. The old man says bitterly "When they can [fire] me here, I wisht somebody'd shoot me."

Candy has 250 dollars compensation for his hand injury, another 50 dollars in the bank, and 50 more coming. His 350 dollars, plus the 100 dollars George and Lennie can save in a month, is enough to become the three men's stake in the future. George at last has money to buy the farm he wants from the old couple that own it.

LAND OF IMMIGRANTS

*In the 1800s, most migrants to the United States settled first in the cities of the East, such as New York, but later generations spread to the West. After the **Civil War** of 1861–1865, and the freeing of black slaves, many African Americans moved from the South to the cities of the North and to the West. By the 1930s, California was the fastest-growing state, drawing in people from across the United States as well as migrants from Mexico, the Philippines, Japan, and China.*

Migrants arrived by ship from Europe to start a new life in the United States.

Steinbeck's farmer-grandparents

Buying a farm was a traditional symbol of immigrant success, and Steinbeck, as "a believer in goodness and the American dream", would have understood this dream. The Steinbeck family had immigrant origins. John's mother's father, Samuel Hamilton, had come from Ireland to Salinas. John learned farm-skills as a boy on his Grandfather Hamilton's farm. His father's father, John Adolph Grosssteinbeck, came to the United States from Germany and he set up as a dairy farmer in California.

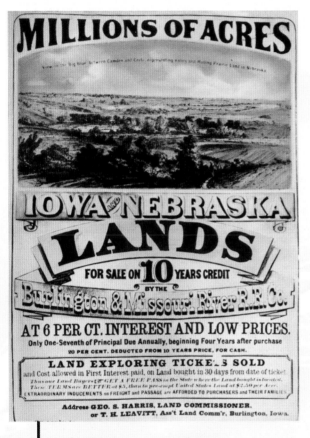

Steinbeck knew from his own family history that people could make the American dream come true. But by the 1930s the Depression seemed to be destroying the dream. When the African-American Crooks listens to the story of George and Lennie's dream, he shares it for a moment. Then he dismisses it as fantasy, a story he's heard before from other hopefuls. "Nobody never gets to heaven," he says, "and nobody gets no land. It's just in their head."

This poster from about 1900 advertises land for sale in the West. Many migrants wanted to buy property and make new lives for their families.

> *I seen hunderds of men come by on the road ... They come, an' they quit an' go on; and every damn one of 'em's got a little piece of land in his head.*

This is how Crooks, in *Of Mice and Men*, sees men like George and Lennie who dream of a patch of land they can call their own. To them, owning land means freedom.

Characters and issues in *Of Mice and Men*

"Guys like us that work on ranches are the loneliest guys in the world," says George, in the opening chapter of the novel. He and Lennie make an odd couple. They first appear, tired and hungry, to camp beside a pool. They wear workers' clothes – jeans and denim coats (in the 1930s jeans were not fashion items). Both wear "black, shapeless hats" and carry blanket rolls, or "bindles", slung over their shoulders. George is "small and quick", while Lennie is huge, "shapeless of face", and walks like a bear.

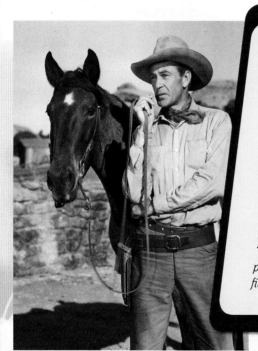

STRONG, SILENT MAN

Slim is "the prince of the ranch, capable of driving ten, sixteen, even twenty mules. . . There was a gravity in his manner . . . all talk stopped when he spoke." The others look up to him, even if he is not drawing a six-gun from his holster. Steinbeck draws on a rich tradition for Slim's character: from the real "Wild West" to the Hollywood western movie, the "strong, silent man'" was idealized – as played by actor Gary Cooper in the 1945 film Along Came Jones.

Innocents on the road

Steinbeck's description of the two men is that they are "two lost souls". They stick together. Like many men on the road, they are lonely and have no families. Lennie once had an Aunt Clara, but she is dead. Now George looks after Lennie, who would find life hard on his own, or most likely be locked up. Most people regarded as "simple-minded" in the 1930s were shut up in special hospitals called asylums, which were more like prisons. George feels the burden of taking care of Lennie, and thinks how simple life would be without him: "If I was alone, I could live so easy." He could stay in a **cat house**, eat in hotels, drink whisky, and play cards or pool. Instead, he tells Lennie in frustration, "I got you!"

Two buddies together

"Buddies" like George and Lennie can be found in many books and films. Examples are Sherlock Holmes and Dr Watson, Laurel and Hardy, and Butch Cassidy and the Sundance Kid. These buddies are two friends, usually male, who live or work together. Often the stronger looks after the weaker. Steinbeck himself had close male friendships. George knows Lennie very well. He knows that a toy mouse will not satisfy Lennie's desire for a pet, and that only a real one will do. Letting Lennie have a pup is a kind gesture, even though he is not sure that Lennie will be able to look after it.

Paul Newman and Robert Redford played two real-life outlaws, Butch Cassidy and The Sundance Kid, in a film that focused on the "buddy-bond" between the two men.

Characters alone

Curley's wife, Candy, and Crooks are also alone or lonely. The bunkhouse men are friendly, though their leader Slim is a loner and a "strong, silent" man who commands respect. Slim understands how things are between George and Lennie. Of Lennie, Slim says simply, "He's a nice fella. Guy don't need no sense to be a nice fella."

Women in the 1930s

Curley's wife is not a "new woman" of the 1930s, except that she knows she has missed out on the developments other women have experienced. After the long campaign by **suffragettes** before World War I, women had won the vote. American women first voted in the presidential election in 1920, and all women over 21 in Britain voted in the 1929 general election. By 1930, younger women, mostly in the big cities, were enjoying new freedom. They were working in shops, factories, and offices. But women usually stayed at home after they married, to care for their home and children.

The Depression was tough for women with families. Men were the main earners so when men lost their jobs it was difficult to manage. Many poor women did part-time work, taking in washing for example, for a little money.

Curley's wife is young, lonely, and bored. She is isolated in a man's world, and her crude husband treats her badly. The ranch hands see the danger: one woman on the ranch, newly married, and with no children. Their main contact with women is in town, where they visit the two local cat houses. They prefer the one where a man can just sit around, enjoying a drink and a chat if that is all he wants.

Female office workers. More women got full-time jobs in the 1920s and 1930s, but women workers were paid less than men, even for the same work.

HOLLYWOOD'S FEMMES FATALES

In the 1930s, Hollywood constantly demanded "new faces" on the screen. Most girls got into films because of their looks rather than acting talent, often starting as dancers or beauty queens. Leading ladies might reach the top through talent and intelligence as well as looks, for example, Bette Davis and Katharine Hepburn, but most got parts through their "sex appeal". They acted like "Femmes Fatales" – enticing, dangerous women.

The wife as a victim

Curley's wife "had full rouged lips and wide-spaced eyes, heavily made up. Her finger-nails were red." This description signals her as a "femme fatale": a woman whose sexuality gets men into trouble. The men call her a "tart", but this is unfair. She is young and lonely. Curley is violent and jealous, and sees her as his possession. She does not even have a name in the novel. Without a job, friends, or independence she is just as disabled as Crooks or Candy. She has no friends to talk to, and ends up in the barn with Lennie because he is the only one around. She talks wistfully of how she might have become a film star if only the right man had whisked her off to Hollywood. In her dream, she might have become a new Jean Harlow. Instead, she married Curley and already regrets it. She becomes a victim.

> *Coulda been in the movies, an' had nice clothes . . . An' I coulda sat in them big hotels, an' had pitchers took of me.*

Curley's wife dreamt of becoming a Hollywood star. Her dream has faded now that she is tied to the ranch, with a husband she does not love.

Studio bosses were always on the lookout for a "new Jean Harlow". The "blonde bombshell" from Kansas was one of Hollywood's biggest stars until her death in 1937, at the age of only 26.

Racial tensions

The only African-American character in *Of Mice and Men* is Crooks. His job is to look after the stable, and the harness for mules, horses, and wagons. Like Candy, he is disabled. "Crooks" may be a nickname, because of his bent back. He lives apart from the white ranch hands, and his isolation represents the alienation and hopelessness of many African Americans in the 1930s.

Living separately

Crooks lives in the harness room, where he keeps some books and magazines to pass the time. He does not sit around the bunkhouse table playing cards with the white men. **Racial segregation** existed in much of the United States, especially in the South. It meant that blacks and whites sat apart on public buses and in restaurants, and went to different schools.

Crooks keeps his distance from the white men, though they are not unfriendly. They respect Crooks for his skills and Candy calls him a "nice fella". Only Slim and the boss have been into his room until first Lennie, and then Candy, wanders in. Crooks would like to believe in George and Lennie's dream, remembering his own childhood: "the white kids came to play at our place, an' sometimes I went to play with them. . ." But he cannot believe it will ever happen, and he tells Lennie bluntly "You're nuts." His is the "voice of doom", preparing the reader for the tragedy that will happen later.

Separate drinking fountains for whites and "coloreds": an example of racial segregration in the Southern states of America at the time *Of Mice and Men* was written.

FOR COLORED ONLY

Fear of accusation

George, Lennie, and Candy dream of freedom, but Crooks' **pessimism** comes from a lifetime of bad experience. As an African-American man who is disabled he carries a double burden. He is safer if he stays apart from the whites. His relationship with Curley's wife is particularly risky. Crooks knows he must be very careful when talking to her: not only because she is married to the boss's son, but also because she is white. She has only to threaten: "You know what I can do if you open your trap", and he is scared. His fear comes from knowing that if she were to accuse him of assault, he might be seized by a **lynch mob**, and hanged from a tree.

A civil rights protest in America in the 1950s, when African-American students enrolled in "whites-only" schools in the South, here confronted by supporters of segregation making a counter-protest.

12 MILLION BLACK VOICES

*African-American writer Richard Wright was critical of black writers who did not "identify with the masses" and use their writing to support **civil rights**. Wright's 1941 book called 12 Million Black Voices was a blast of anger against the sufferings of African Americans in the Depression, and racial discrimination. Despite the fame of black celebrities such as musicians Duke Ellington, Louis Armstrong, and Marian Anderson, and Olympic athlete Jesse Owens, there were still racial barriers in America, and opposition to discrimination fuelled the civil rights marches and new laws of the 1950s–1960s.*

The ideal home

"Some day . . . we're gonna have a little house and a couple of acres . . ." The farm, with its orchard, chickens, a few pigs, and a stream with salmon swimming in it represents paradise to George and Lennie. Just talking about it eases the pain of their daily lives.

The men picture themselves doing as they please, tending the farm, fishing, watching a baseball game or a circus, or having a friend to stay. Interestingly, women do not feature in their vision of the "ideal home".

THE GOOD LIFE

We could "live offa the fatta the lan. . ." dreams Lennie wistfully. Living off the fat of the land meant enjoying the good life – plenty to eat and drink, not too much hard work, and freedom. George and Lennie share the aspirations of many other Americans. Their dream is to buy a small plot of land, and build a farmhouse, as the pioneers did before them.

This 1930s poster was designed to appeal to the "modern woman", eager to make the most of new opportunities in a changing society.

Let Health go with you through the year

Drink Delicious 'OVALTINE' The Beverage for Health

Contented old age

Candy proclaims with battered pride that, "I lost my right hand on this ranch." Now he must face up to old age and disability, for he can no longer keep up with the fitter men, and so has to sweep up. Old age looks bleak, which is why he is so excited by the dream future that is conjured up by George, and why he is ready to pitch in his life savings of 350 dollars to buy a share. Adequate **pensions** in retirement were a long way off for most 1930s citizens. Most people relied on their own savings or hoped their children would support them.

A new mood

George's hopefulness, in spite of his hard life, reflects a changing national mood in the United States. By 1937, the Depression was ending, thanks in part to the New Deal (see page 32). Farmers were becoming more prosperous, as wheat prices rose by three times between 1932 and 1936, and factories were busy again. Films and advertisements pictured the "good life", with its clean, shiny cars, radios, washing machines, vaccuum cleaners, and **iceboxes**.

Not everyone welcomed this shiny, modern **materialism**. Many people, like Steinbeck, looked back with affection to the old-fashioned values of the pioneers who crossed the West. George and Lennie's dream is closer to this traditional picture of the good life, a "little house on the prairie".

Steinbeck distrusted the modern world's fascination with possessions. "If I wanted to destroy a nation, I would give it too much . . .", he wrote in the late 1950s.

The "good life" meant the marvels of science in the home. Labour-saving appliances, like the cleaner advertised here, freed women from the chores familiar to their mothers and grandmothers. This was happening all over the western world.

ADVERTISING THE FUTURE

Advertising was used by business to sell the good life. Poster artists pictured happy, smiling families in "ideal" homes, enjoying all the new comforts of modern life. In the United States, radio stations carried cheery commercials that reassured people that life was good and getting better. Even in the Depression, people with little cash to spend were surrounded by advertisements for new cars, houses in the suburbs, vacuum cleaners, radios, and washing machines.

Writing about a changing world

The first 40 years of the 20th century saw war, unrest, and political upheaval on a global scale. Among the events of these years were: World War I, the Russian Revolution, the break-up of old empires, votes for women, and demands for civil rights for minorities. Few writers could ignore these events.

British writer George Orwell joined other volunteers to fight for the Republican side in the Spanish Civil War of 1936-1939. The socialist communist Republicans eventually lost to General Franco's Nationalists.

NO MORE WANDERING KNIGHTS?

Many writers regretted the passing of a more romantic, heroic age. Sinclair Lewis wrote in Babbit in 1922 that "the Romantic Hero was no longer the wandering knight, the cowpuncher [cowboy], the aviator nor the brave young district attorney, but the great sales manager. . ." Steinbeck was a romantic at heart, and "wandering knights" meant a great deal to him.

Taking up causes

Writers sometimes used their books to campaign for political causes. Many were concerned about the war between two **ideologies**: communism and **capitalism**. Communists believed the government must own all wealth and property and run all businesses. Capitalists believed that people should be free to own wealth and property and run private businesses. The US and western Europe were capitalist. The Soviet Union (USSR) was the world's first communist state. Meanwhile in 1930s Italy and Germany, the **fascist** governments were violently anti-communist. Neither system was **democratic**, and both used **censorship** to silence opposition. When ideologies clashed in Spain, there was a civil war.

Committed writers

Writers such as John Steinbeck and Sherwood Anderson in the United States, and George Orwell in Britain, wrote about the class struggle, and about the effects of the Depression on working people. Anderson, whose books usually had a clear left-wing message, boasted that he was "accepted by working people everywhere as one of themselves." Orwell later became a fierce opponent of Soviet communism, which he ridiculed in his book *Animal Farm*. Both Orwell and Steinbeck feared a growing threat to individual freedom from technology, government control, and materialism. Steinbeck had met socialists and union organizers while researching his 1936 novel *In Dubious Battle*, which is about a strike of orchard workers. It was admired by critics, but had not sold well.

Catch the public interest

Most readers browsing in bookshops picked up best-sellers such as Margaret Mitchell's *Gone With the Wind*. This epic novel about the Civil War won the **Pulitzer Prize** in 1937, and was later made into a blockbuster film. People were interested in politics and social issues, but they did not necessarily want to spend their evenings and weekends reading about them. So, when he sat down to write *Of Mice and Men*, Steinbeck wanted to keep his readers entertained as well as informed.

Joseph Stalin, ruler of the USSR from 1924 until his death in 1953. Despite Stalin's brutality, some 1930s writers believed communism offered a better future.

COMMUNISM – GOOD OR BAD?

*In 1917, communists seized power in Russia, and turned the Russian Empire into the Union of Soviet Socialist Republics (USSR). In the 1930s, Joseph Stalin ruled the USSR as a **dictator**. All Soviet writers had to follow the Communist Party line, or risk prison. Despite Stalin's tyranny, some writers in Europe and the United States still admired the "fair shares for all" ideals of communism. They ignored the truth: that Stalin had millions of people killed or sent to prison camps in icy Siberia.*

The New Deal

The New Deal helped pull the United States out of the Depression. When Franklin Roosevelt took over as US President in March 1933, he told the nation, "This is pre-eminently the time to speak the truth, frankly and boldly." He said Americans must confront honestly "the conditions facing our country today". The "New Deal" was a set of measures to "put America back to work", and Roosevelt drew on many advisers, including black educator Mary McLeod Bethune, and Frances Perkins who, as secretary of labour, was the first woman to hold a top US government post. Roosevelt ended Prohibition, reformed the US banking system, and started huge schemes such as the Tennessee Valley Authority project to generate electricity for poor farmers.

President Roosevelt

*Franklin Delano Roosevelt, 32nd president of the United States, was the only President elected four times. He battled against an attack of **polio** in 1921, which left him unable to walk without support, and narrowly escaped assassination in 1933 just after he had defeated Herbert Hoover to win the presidency. Roosevelt led the United States out of the Depression, and through almost all of World War II. He was re-elected in 1936, 1940, and again in 1944, but died in April 1945, shortly before World War II ended.*

A new era

The New Deal provided **federal** government money for emergency relief to the poor and jobless, as well as funds for new schools, roads, bridges, and dams. Key organizations included the Works Progress Administration, which was renamed the Work Projects Administration (WPA) in 1939. The WPA found jobs for around a million unemployed people a year, and gave work to writers, musicians, artists, and photographers. For example, WPA writers wrote guidebooks for US states, which helped to make Americans more aware of their regional cultures. The Civilian Conservation Corps, providing work for young people, lasted into the 1940s, by which time World War II had begun, and American factories were working flat-out making weapons and war equipment.

Outside the system

Although the New Deal made people aware of the poverty of migrant workers, it did not often help men like George and Lennie. They are outside the system with no regular jobs. They have no mortgages, no loans to repay, and probably do not pay taxes. Their dream is to be independent. George is intelligent, clean, works hard, and causes no trouble in the bunkhouse. He might well earn more in a steady job as a salesman, but he has a country worker's skills, and he has Lennie to look after. Without Lennie, at the end of the story, the reader is left to imagine what the future may hold for George on his own.

None of the characters in *Of Mice and Men* listens to a radio in the bunkhouse. If they had, they might have heard President Franklin D. Roosevelt's "fireside chats". The President used radio to explain to Americans how the New Deal was meant to help them.

Experiments in fact and fiction

The 1930s were a time of experiment in literature and art, especially in the art of documenting modern life. Theatre groups in New York City and elsewhere staged plays based on real events. An example was *Waiting for Lefty,* a play by Clifford Odets about a taxi-drivers' strike. In it, the characters discuss whether President Roosevelt's New Deal will really benefit working people.

Newspapers, and magazines such as *The New Republic*, in the United States, and *New Statesman*, in Britain, dealt with politics in long articles, but editors also saw a way to use photographs to highlight issues of the day. Editors sent journalists and photographers around the country to document the problems of the unemployed during the Depression.

> ## It is an experiment and I don't know how successful. There are problems in it, difficult of resolution.

Steinbeck said this about *Of Mice and Men* as he worked on it in the new house at Los Gatos, California, to which he and his wife Carol moved in the summer of 1936.

Stories in pictures

From 1936, *Life* magazine pioneered the "photo-essay", and other magazines followed their lead, including *Picture Post* in Britain. The New Deal's WPA programme helped photographers show the harsh reality of the Depression. Photos by Margaret Bourke-White and Erskine Caldwell, and by Dorothea Lange and Paul Taylor in their book, *An American Exodus: A Record of Human Erosion*, caused a stir. *Fortune* magazine sent James Agee and Walker Evans to Alabama. When their book was published in 1941 as *Let Us Now Praise Famous Men*, Agee said that he had tried to tell the story of farmers' families "as exactly and clearly" as he could.

Margaret Bourke-White used an advertising billboard as a background to her photo *The American Way* of poor people lining up for a food handout in 1937. The image on the poster, with the confident slogan, provides a contrast to the people standing in line.

The work of the WPA

Dorothea Lange became one of the best-known photographers working with the WPA. She had taken photos of jobless people waiting on the breadline for handouts of food, and was then hired by the state of California to photograph migrant workers. She used their words as captions to her pictures. The impact was so shocking that the state governor set up camps for the homeless, like the one Steinbeck visited (see pages 12–13).

Dorothea Lange's photo *Migrant Mother* became one of the most widely seen images of the Depression.

FILMS ABOUT REAL LIFE

While most films offered escapist entertainment, the cinema also provided information. In the United States, the WPA backed films such as Pare Lorentz's The Plow That Broke the Plains about the Dust Bowl. Steinbeck met Lorentz in 1938, and Lorentz invited him to Hollywood. In Britain, John Grierson and other film-makers made documentary films about British life (one famous film, Night Mail, was about the nightly mail trains).

Vanishing values

"Maybe ever'body in the whole damn world is scared of each other." This is the view of the mule-driver Slim, a man who seems scared of nobody, commenting on why so few men travel alone. Wise and strong, he is the ideal Westerner: "his word was taken on any subject, be it politics or love".

To a writer like Steinbeck, raised in the country, Slim represents a dying tradition. The modern world had little time for the skills of men like Slim, passed down over generations. To his sorrow, Steinbeck could see much of the old California fast vanishing, with cars and trucks replacing horses and mules, and cities with their freeways and factories growing rapidly.

Langston Hughes, pictured here as a bus-boy (table-cleaner in a restaurant), became a key figure in the so-called "Harlem Renaissance" artistic movement. He and other Harlem-based writers wrote from the African-American perspective. Steinbeck also tried to show real American life by writing from his own experiences.

Writing about the real United States

By writing about his home state, Steinbeck believed he could write "truly American" books. He loved the California landscape, and begins *Of Mice and Men* by describing the landscape where wild animals leave tracks around pools, with paths "beaten hard" by boys from the ranches coming to swim and by tramps from the highway looking for water and rest. His love of nature comes across strongly as he describes a natural world that is little touched by humans. The bindlestiffs have nothing to do with new homes, new factories, and new methods of agriculture. The farm that George and Lennie dream about, with its windmill and iron stove, belongs more to the 1800s than the 1900s.

Make-believe landscapes

Other writers also felt uncomfortable in a world changing so quickly. Some invented places to write about. John O'Hara wrote about "Gibbsville", a small town based on his own home town of Pottsville in Pennsylvania. William Faulkner invented Yoknapatawpha County, rooted in his home state of Mississippi. He even drew a map of his imaginary county. Novelists Eudora Welty and Ellen Glasgow, and the poet Allen Tate, wrote about life in southern states, a way of life fast vanishing by the 1930s.

William Faulkner set his novels in a fictional county modelled on Jefferson County, Mississippi.

City writers

Steinbeck seldom wrote about big cities, but other writers used cities as the setting for books about the United States. Langston Hughes wrote about Harlem, the mainly African-American district of New York City, while James Farrell wrote three novels about a young man named Studs Lonigan growing up on the streets of Chicago's South Side. Studs Lonigan became a **popular culture hero** of the Depression years.

THE CHANGING UNITED STATES

The United States was the pace-setter for change in the first half of the 1900s. Americans owned more cars, more telephones, and more radios than anyone else. US cities had the world's tallest buildings: the Empire State Building in New York (then the world's tallest building) was completed in 1931. City life seemed to represent the modern ideal, a landscape changing almost daily.

Rebel and romantic

"It's a rotten and depressing situation here; this isn't the place I knew as a boy." Steinbeck wrote this in a letter to his friend Toby Street in 1936. He had just returned from his trip through the migrant relief camps set up in California. Route 66, the main highway from Oklahoma to California's Central Valley, was crowded with migrant families "in ancient rattling automobiles, **destitute**, hungry and homeless, ready to accept any pay so that they may eat and feed their children." The poor people he had seen were the United States' refugees looking for a fresh start, heading for the Californian farms and ranches that in the past had given jobs to wanderers like George Milton and Lennie Small.

Victims and heroes

What he saw depressed Steinbeck. Though he supported Roosevelt's New Deal, he was not sure that politicians or protesters would in the end do much to change the lives of ordinary people suffering such hardships. Despite the poverty and misery he had seen, he believed a person could change from victim to hero by looking for what he called "hidden treasure". Steinbeck said that in *Of Mice and Men* he wanted Lennie to stand for the "**inarticulate** and powerful **yearnings** of all men". His book was to be about the Depression, and about the United States, but it was to have a wider aim, too. He wanted it to illustrate, through the hopes of simple people, one answer to the problems of modern life.

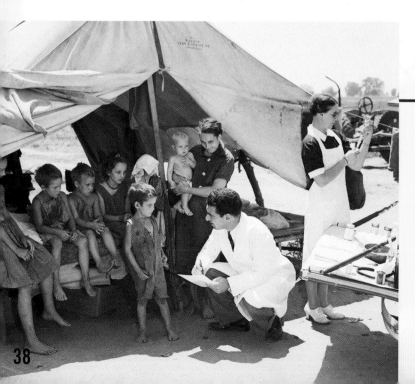

The roads in California were crowded with hungry families, travelling in hope of a job and a place to live. Illness was common.

Treasure-seeking

For George and Lennie, their treasure would be the farm. For a writer, the treasure meant being read and becoming famous. Steinbeck's parents did not live to see him achieve world fame as a novelist. His mother died in 1934, and his father in 1936, just a year after *Tortilla Flat* made Steinbeck's name in 1935.

Steinbeck's success with *Of Mice and Men* came just afterwards, in 1937. That success at first seemed unlikely. Friends who first read Steinbeck's "little book" had expected another blockbuster "strike novel", and instead he had written a very short book about two very ordinary men, one of whom shoots the other at the end of the story.

In this illuminated manuscript from medieval times, the Knights of the Round Table see a vision of the Holy Grail. This ancient story has links to *Of Mice and Men*.

LOOKING FOR THE HOLY GRAIL

In the King Arthur stories (see page 47), knights ride out to have adventures and look for the Holy Grail, the cup used by Christ at the Last Supper with his followers. The quest for the Grail became one of the most powerful stories in Western literature. Steinbeck's story has echoes of these ancient knightly tales. He saw George and Lennie as adventurers on a quest: their "Holy Grail" is the farm they dream of owning.

Writers and rebels

Writers with firmly held political or artistic views often saw themselves as rebels. In 1935, the American Writers' Congress publicly supported the Soviet communist leader Stalin, despite the fact that Stalin was locking up writers and anyone else who opposed him, and had ordered the killing of many thousands of innocent people (see page 31). The Congress did so because its members believed, wrongly as it turned out, that the communists in Russia were building a fairer and more just society than the United States, Britain, or anywhere else in the world. Also, to support Stalin was an act of defiance, so it made the writers feel like rebels.

Sacco and Vanzetti in jail in America. The two Italian immigrants were charged with robbery and murder. Because they said they were anarchists (anti-government), many people felt that they did not get a fair trial. Both men were executed in 1927. The case became a talking point, especially among writers and intellectuals.

Fear of revolution

Steinbeck visited Russia in 1937. He believed in a fairer society, but was not a communist. Anyone who did visit Russia, however, risked being suspected of pro-communist views. Some wealthy Americans feared that workers in the United States were plotting revolution. Steinbeck was told by a friend that two FBI agents (as she guessed they were) came into her Monterey bookshop, and asked odd questions such as: Was this author a communist? What kind of books did he buy? Angry farmers' groups also apparently had Steinbeck's name on lists of communist **sympathizers** because of his support for their poor farmworkers.

Steinbeck took care to stay in the middle of the argument. He thought both sides (communists and capitalists) were just as bad. Not long after he published *Of Mice and Men* he wrote that it was just as silly to believe that "communists are devils who want to steal the little house of the grocery clerk" as it was to go about believing that "industrialists are fat, greedy, cruel beasts who take pleasure in bombing their workers".

Not taking sides

Steinbeck's 1936 novel *In Dubious Battle* is based on a real-life strike by lettuce packers in California. This was the closest Steinbeck came to "taking sides". The book's main character is a union strike organizer who ends up dead. Steinbeck blames both sides – farmers and unions – for the violence. When nothing came of his hopes of turning this book into a film, he started work on a simpler story, *Of Mice and Men*. *Time* magazine later called *Of Mice and Men* "a fairy tale".

This suggests that it was very different to what most readers expected. There is no reference in the story to major modern events. The ranch seems untouched by the outside world. George, Lennie, Candy, Crooks, and Curley's wife are all victims, not rebels. In writing about them and their dreams, Steinbeck was not interested in Californian politics, or in world revolution. He wanted to explore the dreams of ordinary men and women for whom he felt sympathy. "You can't hate men if you know them", he wrote in his journal.

BACKING COMMUNISM

In 1932, a communist called William Z. Foster ran for president of the United States. He attracted support from more than 50 American writers. It was also briefly fashionable for students to join the Communist Party or socialist clubs. This was their way of showing that they were dissatisfied with society, especially the way the poor had suffered during the Depression.

British students carry the hammer and sickle emblem of the Communist Party, to show their support for socialist revolution.

Books as protest

In the 1930s, Stalin banned certain books, and Adolf Hitler burned the works of writers who disagreed with his views. These two dictators hated and feared **free speech**. Many writers felt threatened by the rise of such powerful dictatorships. The world seemed to be becoming a huge economic machine, in which most people were just tiny cogs. Individuality seemed unimportant in this system.

Men or machines?

Steinbeck had read Frank Norris's novel *Octopus*, which was the story of a power-struggle between Californian wheat farmers and railroad bosses. Norris thought that people were shaped by their environment, and had little hope of escaping their fate, an idea loosely based on the theories of naturalist Charles Darwin. Summed up as "the survival of the fittest", this meant that the strong get on, while the weak are trampled underfoot. It was a gloomy view of life and not one that Steinbeck really shared. He believed people could triumph against the odds.

WORKING FOR THE PRESS BARON

In the 1920s, Steinbeck worked for a New York City newspaper, the American. It was one of many papers owned by William Randolph Hearst. Steinbeck was no good as a reporter. He kept getting lost in the city, and he was fired after only a few weeks.

William Randolph Hearst (1863-1951) owned 28 daily newspapers by 1937. The sensational big-headline style favoured in Hearst papers became known as "yellow journalism".

Finding a voice

Steinbeck believed writers could help the poor and weak by making readers and the government aware of their problems. This was possible in the United States and Britain. But in the 1930s, protest writing was very dangerous in communist Russia and Nazi Germany, where anyone criticizing the government was either jailed or executed. After Hitler came to power in Germany in 1933, many writers fled from Germany. In the United States and Britain there was free speech, though many newspapers were controlled by powerful **tycoons**, such as William Randolph Hearst in the United States and Lord Northcliffe in Britain.

Reaching a wider public

Writers could publish their ideas, and protests, in their books. Small publishers, such as Pat Covici who published *Of Mice and Men*, were willing to take a chance on an author with new ideas, even if he or she might not sell many books. Today, large companies usually run book publishing. In the 1930s, there were many smaller firms and small firms helped struggling writers such as Steinbeck.

The first paperbacks, which were much cheaper than hardcover books, proved popular. Penguin Books launched Britain's first paperback series in 1935, and paperback sales quickly grew. Readers could also buy from **book clubs**, such as the Book of the Month Club, which began in the United States in 1926, and the Left Book Club, which started in Britain in 1936. Book clubs issued a range of titles, from detective stories and historical romances to serious political literature, to suit all tastes. So more and more people were reading regularly.

PENGUIN BOOKS

OF
MICE AND MEN

CANNERY ROW

JOHN STEINBECK

FICTION

COMPLETE   UNABRIDGED

1/6

The first Penguin edition of *Of Mice and Men*.

WORTH READING?

Many readers bought magazines. In Of Mice and Men, there are magazines in the bunkhouse, and Whit, one of the men, is thrilled to find one magazine contains a reader's letter sent in by a former workmate. Crooks reads because he is lonely, but thinks books are a "second-best" entertainment. He complains, "S'pose you couldn't go into the bunk house and play rummy [a card game] 'cause you was black. How'd you like that? S'pose you had to sit out here an' read books."

The success of Steinbeck's little book

When *Of Mice and Men* came out in February 1937, the first reactions were mixed, but early in 1938 the Book of the Month Club chose it as a main title. This guaranteed good sales, and it was soon selling 100,000 copies a month.

Life changes

For Steinbeck, sales meant more money coming in. He bought some new furniture and a phonograph to play records on, which he enjoyed putting together from a do-it-yourself kit. After *Of Mice and Men*, he was famous and his life would never be the same again. The "Steinbeck style" was now recognised by readers.

Of Mice and Men told a simple story in plain language. For many, the book showed a United States they had not seen represented in fiction before. They were moved by its compassion, and its message of companionship. George and Lennie own only what they carry on their backs, but their friendship enriches them. Unlike other loners, who "don't belong no place" they have their dream of the farm.

After *Of Mice and Men,* Steinbeck was one of the most successful writers in America. Here he grins cheerfully, holding some of his bestsellers.

On stage

Steinbeck had always hoped to turn *Of Mice and Men* into a stage play or film (he called it a "playable novel"). In May 1937 The Theater Union of San Francisco staged *Of Mice and Men* as a play. For the New York Broadway production, which opened in November 1937, Steinbeck and a New York-based writer and director, George S. Kaufman, altered the text. In the stage play, Curley's wife appears in new scenes, and she fantasizes about being Greta Garbo or Joan Blondell, who were two famous 1930s film stars.

The celebrity and the fuss

After his book became a bestseller, Steinbeck received many letters from readers, and requests for interviews and public appearances. As he was living in a house with no telephone, answering urgent requests often meant time-consuming trips by car to the nearest payphone, which he found irritating. Money from the book's sales paid for a trip to Europe, stopping off in New York City, where as a celebrity author he attended a banquet in honour of Thomas Mann, a refugee author from Nazi

In the barn, Curley's wife allows Lennie to touch her hair, warning him "Don't you muss it up". This photograph comes from the 1992 film of Steinbeck's story. In the stage play, Curley's wife was given more to say.

Germany. He also had several noisy quarrels with his wife as their marriage began to fail. The Steinbecks returned from Europe in time for the opening of the New York stage version of *Of Mice and Men*. Steinbeck then went home to California to work on his next book, *The Grapes of Wrath*, which went on to earn him the Pulitzer Prize in 1940.

THE CRITICAL SEESAW

*Good reviews can make or break a film or play, and affect the sale of novels, too. Newspapers rely for book reviews on professional critics, and often ask other writers or university teachers to assess the latest titles. In 1937, not all reviews of Steinbeck's new novel were favourable. In The Nation, poet and teacher Mark Van Doren called it "an extremely brief novel" in which most of the characters were "**subhuman**". But the New York Times called it "completely **disarming**".*

Steinbeck's later career

Star actor James Cagney said he would like to play George on screen, but when *Of Mice and Men* was first filmed in 1939, Burgess Meredith starred as George, with Lon Chaney Jr. (an actor later noted for horror films) as Lennie. Meredith and Steinbeck became friends and discussed new ventures together.

The novel has remained a top-selling title, despite at times being banned for being immoral and obscene! This happened in 1940 in Australia, for example. One reviewer in *The Catholic World* wrote that, "The first few pages so nauseated me that I couldn't bear to keep it in my room overnight." Despite such comments, *Of Mice and Men* is now studied in many schools. Steinbeck defended his choice of language in 1939, saying "For too long the language of books was different from the language of men."

After *Of Mice and Men*

Steinbeck was offered work as a writer by film producers in Hollywood where F. Scott Fitzgerald, Nathanael West, and other writers were already working. At first he said no, though he did write film scripts later. During World War II (1939–1945) he spent five dangerous months in Europe, as a journalist, and was impressed by stories told to him by Londoners of their experiences during the Blitz, when German bombers pounded Britain. He wrote a wartime film and pieces for newspapers, which were often first-hand accounts of talks with ordinary soldiers.

By the 1940s, Steinbeck was wealthy and able to travel the world by ship and plane. He was frequently recognized wherever he went. Yet praise from critics was often missing.

Ideas like rabbits

After World War II, Steinbeck continued to be a successful novelist through the 1950s, by which time he, Hemingway, and Faulkner were the United States' top writers. All three won the Nobel Prize for literature (see page 49). Yet Steinbeck probably got the least attention, certainly from university professors, perhaps because he ranged widely in his writing from comedy to politics. "Ideas are like rabbits", he told a journalist, "you get a couple, and learn how to handle them and pretty soon you have a dozen."

As ideas continued to flow, he enjoyed the business of writing – getting up early, sharpening pencils, and typing or dictating his words. He wrote more novels, not all well received, as well as film scripts, and journalism. His main interest remained the United States and its people. In 1948, he had revisited Russia, this time with the photographer Robert Capa, who was famous for his wartime battlefield pictures. In *A Russian Journal*, Steinbeck noted the curiosity of Russians about the United States, adding "America is a very difficult country to explain. There are many things about it we don't understand ourselves."

Bomb damage in London after an air raid in 1941. During World War II, Steinbeck spent time in Britain, reporting on people's reaction to the dangers and terrors of war.

THE ARTHUR CONNECTION

Steinbeck wanted to retell in modern English the legends of King Arthur, as told by Sir Thomas Malory, who lived from around 1400 to 1470. He thought Malory was the first great novelist in English, because of the way he got inside the characters. In a letter written in 1957, Steinbeck explained, "A novelist not only puts down a story, but he is the story. He is each one of the characters in a greater or a less degree." If this is true, a little of Steinbeck must be in the characters who appear in Of Mice and Men.

Steinbeck and the modern world

Was Steinbeck a pessimist? After George and Candy find the body of Curley's wife, George knows the farm will never be his. It was just a story to tell to Lennie. "I think I knowed from the very first . . . He [Lennie] usta like to hear about it so much I got to thinking maybe we would", he says sadly.

Steinbeck in his later years was a rather gloomy figure. In 1960, he travelled in the southern states, visiting Texas and Louisiana, where he was shocked by the persistent racism, and depressed by the materialism he saw in US society. He wrote to Pat Covici that although the poverty of the 1930s had gone, in its place was "a sickness, a kind of wasting disease". He was sad to think that, "the nation has become a discontented land". Steinbeck did not like modern America, writing that Americans had "too many THINGS".

STEINBECK AND VIETNAM

When the war in Vietnam was at its height, many writers criticized the United States' involvement in the conflict. Protest groups looked for Steinbeck's support for an anti-war petition. Though he disliked the war, especially the bombing of Vietnam, he refused to sign. He wrote to President Johnson's press secretary that "The Vietnam War is troublesome . . . but I don't sign anything I don't write."

Women protest during an anti-war march in 1965, when opposition to the Vietnam War was growing in the United States. The rights and wrongs of the war bitterly divided Americans.

Nobel Prizewinner

In 1962, John Steinbeck was awarded the Nobel Prize for Literature. The *New York Times* commented that he had written his best books 20 years or more ago, and questioned his relevance to the modern world. Steinbeck took comfort in his belief that ordinary readers mattered more than journalists or university professors. He refused most other honours, but he did accept the Presidential Medal of Freedom in 1964.

Last years

Steinbeck was saddened by the deaths of his publisher and editor Pat Covici, in 1964, and of his sister Mary in 1965. He wrote less and less. In 1967 he visited Vietnam, where his son John was serving in the US Army during the Vietnam War. By now living on Long Island, New York, he was a sick man suffering from a heart condition and breathing problems, unable to go fishing or work in his garden. He died on 20 December 1968, and his ashes were taken back to California.

Steinbeck accepts the Nobel Prize in 1962. The award was international recognition of his stature as a writer.

THE NOBEL PRIZES

Swedish industrialist Alfred Nobel, inventor of the explosive dynamite, left money to fund the Nobel Prizes, first awarded in 1901. The original prizes were for physics, chemistry, physiology or medicine, literature, and for furthering international peace. A sixth prize, for economics, was awarded from 1969. Winners of the Literature prize have included Sinclair Lewis (1930), William Faulkner (1949), Ernest Hemingway (1954), and Steinbeck (1962).

TIMELINE

1902	John Steinbeck born at Salinas, California, on 27 February.
1903	First flight by Orville and Wilbur Wright.
1914-18	World War I – 1914 ends the 'golden age' of American farming.
1916	Number of automobiles in the United States reaches 3.5 million, compared with only 8,000 in 1900.
1917	Communist revolution in Russia overthrows the Tsar (emperor).
1919	Steinbeck graduates from Salinas High School and starts at Leland Stanford Junior University (later Stanford University). During vacations he works on farms and ranches.
1920	US census returns show a majority living in towns. US women get the vote. Prohibition begins.
1925	Steinbeck leaves college and tries his luck in New York City as a reporter, but is fired. He returns to California in 1926, and takes a job at Lake Tahoe, living in a cabin.
1926	Trade unions organize the first, and only, General Strike of workers in Britain.
1927	"Talking pictures" are a hit, with *The Jazz Singer*. Charles Lindbergh flies solo across the Atlantic Ocean.
1928	Steinbeck moves to San Francisco.
1929	Wall Street Crash – US stock market collapses and many investors are ruined. The Depression begins.
1930	Steinbeck marries Carol Henning.
1931	Empire State Building is opened in New York City.
1933	About 13 million Americans are now out of work as the Depression becomes worse. Adolf Hitler becomes leader of Nazi Germany.
1933	Roosevelt succeeds Hoover as US President and brings in the New Deal. Joseph Stalin begins a "purge" of the Communist Party in the USSR, getting rid of opponents.
1933	National Industrial Recovery Act becomes law in the United States. Prohibition is ended. Tennessee Valley Authority is set up.
1935	Second New Deal in the United States; the Social Security Act improves pension rights for the elderly. Wagner Act encourages more workers to join trade unions.
1935	*Tortilla Flat* is Steinbeck's first success as a writer.
1937	*Of Mice and Men* is published.

KEY	World history
	Local/national history (USA)
	Author's life
	Of Mice and Men

1937	Average woman's yearly wage in the United States is US$500, half that of a man.
1939	Spanish Civil War ends. World War II begins in Europe.
1940	Winston Churchill becomes Britain's prime minister. The Blitz on London begins.
1941	United States enters World War II, after Japanese naval planes bomb Pearl Harbor in Hawaii.
1942	Steinbeck writes *The Moon is Down*, a wartime **propaganda** novel about occupied Norway. He and Carol divorce.
1943	Steinbeck marries his second wife, Gwyndolyn Conger, with whom he has two sons.
1945	President Roosevelt dies, and is succeeded by Harry S Truman. World War II ends.
1947	Start of 'anti-communist scares' in the United States. Film-makers and writers accused of pro-communist leanings are called before the Un-American Activities Committee.
1948	Steinbeck divorces Gwyndolyn.
1950	Steinbeck marries for the third time, to Elaine Anderson.
1952	Steinbeck writes the script for the film *Viva Zapata!*
1954	US Supreme Court rules school segregation (separate schools for blacks and whites) in the South to be unconstitutional.
1955	Steinbeck's novel *East of Eden* is filmed, starring the young actor James Dean.
1962	Steinbeck is awarded the Nobel Prize for Literature.
1963	Assassination of President John F. Kennedy. Civil Rights campaigners stage a "freedom march" in Washington D.C.
1964	US Civil Rights Act bans race discrimination in jobs, voting registration and public housing.
1965	First US troops arrive to fight in Vietnam; there are soon mass protests against US involvement in the Vietnam War.
1968	Steinbeck dies on 20 December, in New York City.

FURTHER INFORMATION

The edition used in the writing of this book is *Of Mice and Men*, John Steinbeck (Penguin Modern Classics, 2000)

Other works by John Steinbeck

Tortilla Flat (Covici-Friede, 1935)
In Dubious Battle (Covici-Friede, 1936)
The Red Pony (Covici-Friede, 1937)
The Grapes of Wrath (Viking Press, 1939)
Cannery Row (Viking Press, 1945)
The Pearl (Viking Press, 1947)
East of Eden (Viking Press, 1952)
The Acts of King Arthur and His Noble Knights (Farrar, Straus & Giroux, 1976)
The stage version of *Of Mice and Men*, in three acts, New York Dramatists Service
    1937 (Warner Chappell Plays, 1943)
Once There Was a War (Steinbeck's wartime journalism) (Mandarin, 1990)

Books about Steinbeck, the 1930s, and *Of Mice and Men*

Gaff, Jackie: *20th Century Design: 20s and 30s* (Heinemann Library, 1999)
Parini, Jay: *John Steinbeck* (Heinemann Library, 1994)
Steinbeck, Elaine and Wallsten, Robert (eds): *Steinbeck: A Life in Letters* (Viking, 1975)
Mailer, Norman: *American Dream* (Dial, 1961)
Ross, Stewart: *The Great Depression* (Evans Publishing, 1997)
Senall Isaacs, Sally: *The History of America: The Rise to World Power*, (Heinemann Library, 1999)

Steinbeck / 1930s websites

The 1930s in print and media:
www.eyewitnesstohistory.com/snprelief
www.spartacus.schoolnet.co.uk/REVhistory1930s
The National Steinbeck Center:
www.steinbeck.sjsu.edu
For pictures of Steinbeck's California:
www. caviews.com/john.htm
For quotations from Steinbeck ("search for Steinbeck"):
www.brainyquote.com
**For a visual tour of Steinbeck's homes, visit the John Steinbeck
Pacific Grove website:**
www.93950.com/steinbeck
For more on Nobel Prize winners:
www.almaz.com/nobel/literature/

Films

Tortilla Flat (1942)
Directed by Victor Fleming, starring John Garfield, Hedy Lamarr,
and Spencer Tracy.
Of Mice and Men (1939, 1999)
The first version was directed by Lewis Milestone, and starred Burgess Meredith
and Betty Field. The 1999 film was directed by Gary Sinese, who also played
George, with John Malkovich as Lennie.
The Red Pony (1949)
Directed by Lewis Milestone, starring Robert Mitchum and Myrna Loy.
The Grapes of Wrath (1940)
Directed by John Ford, and starring Henry Fonda, Jane Darwell,
and John Carradine.
East of Eden (1955)
Directed by Elia Kazan, starring James Dean and Julie Harris.

GLOSSARY

bindlestiff slang term for a casual worker, travelling from job to job carrying his possessions in a bundle

book club business selling books, usually monthly, to subscribers

bunkhouse place where ranch workers eat and sleep

capitalism economic system based on a free market in goods and capital (money and property)

cat house American slang for a brothel, where prostitutes work

censorship controlling media (books, films, plays, free speech)

civil rights the right of every person to fair and equal treatment from the law, and from his or her fellow-citizens. The civil rights movement in the USA in the 1950s–60s was aimed at ending racial discrimination and winning equal treatment in voting, housing, education and public life generally for all racial groups.

Civil War the war between the Northern (Union) and Southern (Confederate) states of American, fought over the issues of slavery and states' rights from 1861 – 1865

class struggle conflict between the three main groups in society (upper, middle, and working class)

communism political and economic system based on the ideas of Karl Marx who argued for the common ownership of land and property

consumer boom period of prosperity when people spend freely on goods from shops

democratic political system where people can vote and a majority wins

Depression beginning in 1930, a time of unemployment and hardship in the United States and Europe

destitute having no possessions

disarming having the charm to win over doubters or critics

Dust Bowl ecological catastrophe that struck the Mid West of the United States in the 1930s, ruining many farmers

Emergency Relief Organization organization set up to help with a specific emergency

fascism political system based on dictatorship by a strong leader that began in Italy in the 1920s and spread to Germany, Spain, and other countries

federal type of government where several states are joined together, but still allowed to make their own state rules

free speech freedom to say or write anything, without fear of persecution

goad prod, urge or drive: a goad is a pointed stick used by animal drivers

icebox kitchen refrigerator/freezer

ideologies ideas, opinions and beliefs, set out as teachings, for example in a book

immigrant person who enters one country from another, with the aim of settling permanently

inarticulate unable to express oneself clearly

left-wing term that describes socialist ideas on how society should be organized

lynch mob people who took the law into their hands, hunting down suspected criminals (often black and often innocent)

manuscript original version of a book, before it is printed

materialism belief that what matters in life are things rather than ideas or feelings

migrant person who travels either to settle in a different place, or from place to place to find work

Nobel Prize award presented annually to people for achievements in arts, science, and international affairs, named after Alfred Nobel

pension regular payment to someone who has retired from work or cannot work because of ill-health or injury

pessimism the belief that things are getting worse, not better

pioneer person who is among the first to do something

polio short for poliomyelitis, a disabling disease that could leave a person paralysed for life

popular culture hero a fictional character (such as a cartoon strip hero or a character in a film or novel) who is known and instantly recognized by most people

prosperity wealth and success

Prohibition measures introduced in the United States from 1920–1933 to ban the making and selling of alcoholic drinks. It led to widespread law-breaking.

propaganda using the media to promote a particular belief or viewpoint, including "spinning" a news story and distorting facts

Pulitzer Prize US awards for writing and music, established in 1917 with money left by the Hungarian-born publisher Joseph Pulitzer

racial segregation separation of black and white people through laws requiring them to use separate schools, buses, restaurants, and washrooms

ranch hands workers on a ranch

Silicon Valley name given to Santa Clara County in California where electronics-based industries developed rapidly from the 1970s, based on computer chips (made of silicon)

socialist relating to the belief that the state should control the economy, to bring about social justice and fairer shares of national wealth

stock right of ownership in a business, in the form of share certificates, which can be bought and sold by investors using a market called a stock exchange

strike workers' action against their employer, by refusing to work until a dispute is settled

subhuman less than human, brutish – usually a derogatory term

suffragette campaigner for votes for women in the late 1800s and early 1900s

sympathizers people who support or are in sympathy with a cause or idea put forward by others

trade union organization of workers to protect workers' rights, bargain for improved wages and conditions with employers, and provide benefits for its members

tycoon business leader with great wealth and power

tyrant a boss or ruler who has complete power, tolerates no opposition, and who dominates other people cruelly or unfairly

Wall Street Crash name given to the collapse of prices on the New York Stock Exchange in 1929

yearnings longings or desires

INDEX